Avery's Dream
"Jesus is Alive"

Pearl Robinson

2

I want to thank Vox Illustration for the awesome work they did with bringing my story to life through heartfelt Illustrations. May God forever bless this company who worked with me and quickly made the changes as I requested them.

Introduction

Avery's Dream "Jesus is Alive" is written for the sole purpose of teaching the children about the life of Jesus. I spent ten years working in my church's children's ministry; I taught children about Jesus. I led children to Christ. I believe that teaching children about Jesus when they are small can be a blessing and rewarding for the children and parents. This book is an easy and simple book to read to children, or the children can read and learn about Jesus themselves. In Avery's Dream, "Jesus is Alive," you will find lots of colorful illustrations that bring the story alive. This book is written for children ages 4-7. I believe that this is the perfect bedtime story to read to children. My desire is for this book to bring the family unity back. With technology evolving the way it is, this has separated the family. However, I believe technology can also be a blessing for children who can read Christian books for themselves as an E-book. It is my prayer that children will put their faith in Jesus as the result of hearing or reading this book. Blessings!

Little Avery sat on her bed, waiting for her
mother to tell her a story.

Avery got tired of waiting, she decided to lay down and wait on her mother. Shortly afterward, she fell asleep.

Meanwhile, her mother was busy in the
kitchen, cleaning and preparing lunch for

9

the next day. She totally forgot that Avery was waiting to hear a story about Jesus. When she realized the time, she rushed to Avery's room, but she was asleep. Avery's mother was upset at herself for not telling her daughter the most important story ever told. She kissed little Avery on her forehead and whispered to her "sweet dreams."

After falling into a deep sleep, Avery began

to dream. In her dream, she saw Jesus as

He stood talking to her and some other children.

Then He sat talking with Avery, her

brother, and the other children. She was so

excited to see Jesus because she had so many questions to ask Him.

Avery and the other children were enjoying their time with Jesus. He made them laugh. Jesus told them how much he loved them.

After a while, the other children went to

play. Avery was excited to be alone with

Jesus. Her little brother decided to stay with her.

She told Jesus how she wanted to know all
about His life. She told Him that her

mother was going to tell her His story, but she fell asleep. The little girl told Jesus about all the questions she had to ask Him. Jesus sat down and asked Avery, "What questions do you have for me, my child?"

She replied, "My first question is, can my little brother sit with us?"

"Yes," Jesus replied.

Avery said to Jesus, "I've heard my mother talk about you, and I also heard about you at church."

Jesus asked, "what have you heard about me?"

Avery said, "I heard that you were born in a
filthy stable where animals live." "Some say

your crib was a manger." She continued saying, "It was cold, so your mother wrapped you in swaddling clothes." "Someone also told me you were born to die." "Why?"

Jesus replied, "Yes, it is all true." "I was born in a stable where the animals live." "After my birth, my mother wrapped me in warm clothing and put me in a manger," and "Yes, I was born to die." "I will die for the world one day because I want you and everyone to have everlasting life." "I want everyone to come to Heaven to live with me."

Avery was sad to hear that Jesus had to die.

She stared at Jesus and asked Him, "Why do you have to die?"

"You are my friend, and I don't want you to die." Then she asked, "What is everlasting life?" "If you have to die for me to have it, then I don't want to have everlasting life."

Jesus reached out and hugged Avery,
assuring her that she didn't have to be

afraid. He told her that everyone's body would die one day, and when they die, He desires that everyone go to Heaven. He explains to her that everlasting life is to live in Heaven with Him forever. "My child, everlasting life means life after death." "Everyone who put their faith in Me lives forever," said Jesus.

Avery smiled and replied, "But I am living,

I'm alive, Jesus!" "Can't you see?" "My brother is too!" "So, you don't have to die!" "Please don't die!"

Jesus said to her, "My precious child, I know you are alive." "I am too." "But for you, and all the people who put their faith in Me to live forever, I must die."

Then Avery said, "But Jesus, who told you that you had to die?" "I think whoever is telling you this is being mean to you."

Jesus replied, "My Father, who is in Heaven, said I had too." "Because He loves you and all the other people, I must die for others to live forever as I will."

Avery said, "Jesus, you mean you will die for me, and when I die, I get to live with you

always in Heaven?" "Jesus, you are so
kind." "No one never died for me."

Jesus replied, "Yes, my little one." "I will do
this because I love you." Then Avery asked,
"Is your Father okay with you dying for us?"
"I think He will miss you when you die. I
know I will miss you."

"Yes, My Father is okay with me dying for
the world." "It is my Father's will that I
die." "I have to obey Him because He is my
Father." "Therefore, I must die for all,"
Jesus replied.

Avery asked Jesus, "Who is going to kill
you?" "How will you die?"

Again, she explained to Jesus how sad she
was and that she didn't want to be with

Him when He died. She asked Jesus, "Is
your mother okay with what you are doing?"

Jesus replied, "Yes, my mother knows about

my death. She understands that I have to

die for the sins of the whole world. I will be beaten and made to carry a cross up a hill to be nailed to it.

Once I am nailed to the cross, I will die after a few hours."

Avery said to Jesus, "Sin?" "What is sin?" "I don't understand."

Jesus smiled and said, "My precious little one, do you always listen to your parents?" "Do you tell them the truth all the time?"

"No, sir, I don't." "Sometimes, I tell my mother I ate my vegetables when I put them in the trash." She continued telling Jesus how sometimes her little brother doesn't tell the truth either.

Jesus said, "You see my precious one; those are the sins that I must die for because I want you to live with me." "If I don't die, you and the whole world will never be free from sin."

"Jesus, you are so nice." Avery said, "I don't think I could die for anyone." "The only sad thing is when you die, I will never see you again, and knowing this makes me cry."

Jesus said, "Don't cry." "There's something else I must tell you." "When I die, I won't stay dead on the cross." "I will come back to life."

Avery was amazed at what Jesus said.

"Wow!" said Avery. She closed her eyes with

joy in her heart, Then she said, "How can you do that?" Can you do magic?"

Jesus explains to Avery that He doesn't do magical things. He told her that His Father has the power over life and death, and His Father will raise Him from the dead. "Where is your Father?" Avery asked.

Jesus said, "My Father lives in Heaven." "

He watches over all the other people in the world."

"Oh, no, Jesus!" "You mean He can see me when I do bad things?" Avery replied.

"Yes, child, my Father sits high, but He looks low." "He sees all things." "He sees what people do, where they go, and when people sin."

"Jesus, may I ask you a question?" says Avery?

Jesus replied, "Yes, you may."

"I don't have a Father, can He be my Father too?" "I promise I will be good if He says yes," she said.

"Yes, my little one," said Jesus. "My Father is your Father too; all children have a special place in My Father's heart." "He doesn't want anyone to keep children from coming to Him."

Avery's heart filled with joy at His reply. She continued by asking, "Jesus, when you die and take my sins away, will I sin again?"

Jesus replied, "Yes, you will because you are not perfect." "However, when I go to the cross and die for the sins of the world, you can ask for forgiveness of your sins." "I will talk to my Father about forgiving you, and He will forgive you when you ask Him to forgive you in My name." "He wants you to do the right thing always."

"Jesus," said little Avery, "What will happen to me if I do other sins?"

"My child, sin does not make my Father happy." "He wants you to be good, listen to your mother, and love everybody."

"Jesus, "does this mean I have to love my little brother?" "He gets me into trouble all the time."

"Yes, my precious little one." "You have to love your brother too." "You are his big sister, and you can teach him not to sin."

"I love you Jesus," "I don't want to make your Father mad." "I promise I will be good, and I will love my little brother." Avery hugs her little brother.

"Good, my child, doing what's right will make my Father happy," said Jesus.

"Jesus," said Avery. "When you die and come back alive, where will you go?"

Jesus replied, "I will go back to Heaven to be with my Father." "I will sit to the right hand of my Father on the throne. I will watch over everyone.

With tears in her eyes, Avery asked Jesus, "Can I go with you?"

Jesus hugs her and tells her, "Not now, but I am going to prepare you a special room when I go back to Heaven."

Then Avery asked Jesus, "How will I talk to you when you leave?" "Will I be alone?"

"No, my dear child," Jesus replied. "When I go back to Heaven, I won't leave you alone." "I will leave my Spirit to live in all who believe in me." "They must believe that I died and came back alive," said Jesus.

"You will Jesus?" Avery asked.

"Yes," Jesus replied. "I will live in you." "I will teach you right from wrong, and I will help you make the right choices."

"You will always have hope when you believe in Me." "I must go back to My Father now."

Jesus stood up while Avery and her little brother told Him goodbye, and how much they loved Him. Jesus said, "I love both of you, also." "I will miss you," Avery said. Afterward, she closed her eyes and prayed for Jesus.

Then she said, "I promise to tell all my friends about the good news you shared with me." "Bye-bye, Jesus."

Jesus said, "Goodbye." Then He went
back to Heaven through the clouds
while Avery and the others watched.

Little Avery woke up so excited with a smile on her face. She couldn't wait to tell her mother all about her dream.

She quickly ran down the hall, then into her mother's room, screaming while she was sleeping. "Mommy, I dreamed of Jesus! He is alive! He's in Heaven."

She sat on her mother's bed and shared her
dream about the good news of Jesus Christ,

who was born to die for the sins of the world. Avery said, "Mommy, I saw Him." "He spoke to me." "Malachi and I sat on His lap as He told His story."

Avery's mother had a puzzled look on her face because she knew little Avery was telling her the truth.

Avery's mother said to her, "You are a special child because Jesus appeared to you in a dream. "You are blessed to have had an encounter with our Lord and Savior, Jesus Christ." The two sat on her mother's bed while Avery told her mother the story of Jesus.

Her mother listened carefully to Avery. There was no doubt in her mind that Jesus appeared to her little girl in a dream.

"Mommy," Avery said; "Jesus also promised to watch over us always."

Jesus watches over the children as they played. Avery learned that children have a special place in Jesus's heart.

Matthew 19:14 NKJV "But Jesus said, "Let the little children come to Me, and do not forbid them; for of such is the kingdom of heaven.""

May God bless this book and all who take
the time to read it to a child. May God also
bless the children who will read this book or
listen to it in Jesus name. Amen!